# Stencil Me In

# Stencil Me In

## Marthe Le Van

## LARK BOOKS

A Division of Sterling Publishing Co., Inc.
New York / London

Editor
**Larry Shea**

Assistant Editor
**Mark Bloom**

Art Director
**Kathleen Holmes**

Photographer
**Stewart O'Shields**

Cover Designer
**Eric Stevens**

Stencil Motifs
**Diana Light**
**Orrin Lundgren**

Library of Congress Cataloging-in-Publication Data

Le Van, Marthe.
  Stencil me in / Marthe Le Van. -- 1st ed.
      p. cm.
  Includes index.
  Stencil work.
  ISBN 978-1-60059-252-2 (alk. paper)
  I. Title.
  TT270.L425 2008
  745.7'3--dc22
                                        2008018519

10 9 8 7 6 5 4 3 2


Published by Lark Books, A Division of Sterling Publishing Co., Inc.
387 Park Avenue South, New York, NY 10016

Text © 2008, Lark Books
Photography © 2008, Lark Books, except pages 11, 12, 15, 17,
19–25, 27 © Jupiterimages Corporation

Distributed in Canada by Sterling Publishing, c/o Canadian Manda Group,
165 Dufferin Street, Toronto, Ontario, Canada M6K 3H6

Distributed in the United Kingdom by GMC Distribution Services, Castle Place,
166 High Street, Lewes, East Sussex, England BN7 1XU

Distributed in Australia by Capricorn Link (Australia) Pty Ltd., P.O. Box 704,
Windsor, NSW 2756 Australia

If you have questions or comments about this book, please contact:
Lark Books
67 Broadway
Asheville, NC 28801
828-253-0467

Manufactured in China

ISBN 13: 978-1-60059-252-2

For information about custom editions, special sales, premium and corporate
purchases, please contact Sterling Special Sales Department at 800-805-5489
or specialsales@sterlingpub.com.

# Contents

# ANYONE CAN STENCIL!

Toss out your easel, set aside your sketch pad, and abandon your preconceived notions about painting: It's time to stencil, and things are gonna get a little crazy.

If you've never painted before or don't really consider yourself an artist, have no fear. Included in this book, you'll find 28 actual stencils to play with, as well as more than 100 ideas of where you can use them. You'll learn how to turn thrift-store-cheap into thrift-store-chic by stenciling onto a blazer, jeans, or even tights. Your kid will be super cool at school when his lunchbox features a retro robot. A simple chandelier silhouette on a stretched canvas makes wall art that's really attractive (not to mention fast and easy!). All you need are the stencils included here, a few supplies, and some paint. Sometimes you won't even need the paint—you can use these stencils to help you embroider a custom cuff, add wax to a candle, or frost cupcakes to make them truly unique!

Because the concept of stenciling is so basic—cut out a template and paint through the openings—the technique can result in an endless variety of looks, from precious and pretty to dark and graphic. Everyone from street artists to home makeover mavens is stenciling up a storm these days.

Stenciling is all about customizing, so don't be afraid to follow your creativity. You can use just part of a stencil, or you can combine two, three, or four stencils in new and exciting ways. Experiment with mixing and layering colors. Explore making and cutting your own stencils. In the back of the book, you'll find pages with the 28 featured stencil motifs that you can enlarge or reduce to create designs in whatever size you'd like. But don't limit yourself to the stencils found here. Using simple materials such as contact paper or even heavy paper, you can cut stencils of your own design, or you can copy or print designs and images and make stencils of those. You can even take photographs of your friends and family members and make great pop art portraits they will love.

If you're someone who cares about both crafting and our planet, you'll find that stenciling is a great way to give new life to old objects. Take flea-market paintings, clothes with regrettable stains, or hand-me-down furniture, and add a stencil to refresh and recycle them. You can transform an entire room by stenciling on the walls, or create a party theme by stenciling your invitations, dinner menu, coasters, and table-cloth to match. Customize old T-shirts with stencils of your favorite musicians, shapes, or animals. Stenciling can give the same type of look as a screenprinting, but it is far easier and more accessible for most of us. What's more, stencils themselves are reusable: with proper care, you can create projects with the same stencil again and again. It's the ultimate "green" craft!

Stenciling is an easy, totally DIY process that can immediately make a bold impact on your things and in your life. Once you get going, I'm sure you'll agree that the possibilities are endless. Our suggestions should serve as your inspiration and starting point; follow your stenciling whims wherever they may take you.

# The Simple Facts

## Stencil: a Noun & a Verb

First, you take a stencil (noun). Place it against a surface: a wall, cabinet, placemat, handbag, glass, mouse pad, or just about anything you can think of. Then apply some paint to stencil (verb) the surface. In just a few minutes, you'll create a striking design that will turn a drab object into an eye-catching one, or transform an ordinary room into something special. Quite a trick.

Let's back up a second. What *is* a stencil? It's a thin piece of plastic film or other impervious material with certain areas cut out in a design. When you place it flat against the surface to be stenciled, paint can only pass through the cutout areas.

Just a few basic types of stencils will fulfill your stenciling needs. *Single overlay* stencils require only one stencil to create the complete image. *Multiple overlay* stencils take two or more stencils—typically with each using a different color—to compose the full picture. A *silhouette* stencil produces a single solid shape, like those old-fashioned cutouts of a person's profile. It's the simplest kind of stencil. More elaborate single overlay stencils include connective parts known as bridges or ties that translate into gaps in the stenciled image. These bridges add shapes and detail to your design.

Another type of stencil is a *reverse stencil*. It's designed so that the applied paint creates an image where the background (or negative space) is painted and the shape of your object stays the original color of the surface. To make a regular stencil, you cut away the parts of the image you want to see in the end. For a reverse stencil, you take away everything that is *not* part of the design. It's like what Michelangelo (who should know) said about the trick of sculpting—just remove everything from the block of marble that is *not* part of the sculpture.

The stencils you'll find here are the single overlay variety. You can create more complex images by overlaying multiple stencils, but this book features the bold, contemporary, graphic look of single stencils and silhouettes. These stencils are great for beginners. You'll find that working with them is easy, fast, and fun.

# Things You'll Need...

You can find most essential stenciling supplies—and there aren't all that many really—at local craft and hobby stores. If you are stenciling a room, you may need to look for a few tools—such as a level, plumb line, or tape measure—at a hardware or home-improvement store. As you gain experience and become even more stencil-happy, you can search stencil catalogs and online sites for a wide variety of detailed stencils, high-quality brushes, and other accessories.

## ...to Make the Stencil

Stencils can be made from a variety of materials. Commercial stencils are cut from a sturdy plastic called polyester film or polyethylene. This material is extremely durable and cleans up easily; if you care for them properly, such stencils can last for years and create a design dozens of times. Most commercial stencils are laser cut from 5-mil or 7-mil film. Laser cutting makes it possible to create fine, intricate designs.

You can cut your own stencils from polyethylene and other plastics or acetates. Buy blank sheets of polyester film at a craft and hobby store and look in the quilting section for large sheets of template plastic. You can also use overhead acetate (the sheets used with overhead projectors) or X-ray film for making templates.

Thinner plastics are easier to cut, and they're great for stenciling around a corner or on a curved surface. You can also print your pattern with a household printer and ordinary paper and laminate it before cutting. Watch out, though: Thinner materials tear more easily—especially those with a complicated design—and won't stand up to as many uses. This might not be a problem if you're making a one-of-a-kind (or three- or four-of-a-kind) piece.

The transparency of plastic gives it a big advantage when it comes to tracing or cutting out a design, or when you need to align a stencil with a part of the design you've already painted. But plastic is not the only way to go. Some stencils are made from brass—not known for its see-through qualities. You can also cut stencils out of materials like card stock, poster board, or craft foam, which are rigid and strong enough for accurate stenciling but not flexible enough for bending around corners or curves.

If you're cutting stencils from any material that is somewhat absorbent, you'll want to cover it with sealant or a waterproofing chemical. You can treat just about any thick paper with linseed oil to make it waterproof. Other materials you can use to make stencils include vinyl, contact paper, and freezer paper.

## ...to Make the Cut

When cutting out your own stencil designs, be sure to use a sharp *craft knife*. An older or blunt blade will slow the job, make it more difficult, and fail to provide the fine, sharp edges you want.

If you plan to create a lot of stencils, consider buying a *stencil cutter*. It's a tool with an electrically heated tip that you hold like a pen. For thicker plastic, a stencil cutter works faster and easier than a knife. You do have to be careful to move the cutter at an even pace to avoid melting a wider swath of plastic than you want.

## ...to Make It Stick

Before you pull out the paintbrushes, use one of the following items to make sure your stencil stays firmly in place.

### Painter's Tape

Applying painter's tape (also called masking tape) is an easy way to keep a stencil in place. Look for low-adhesive tape, because it adheres well enough to hold the stencil but won't mar the surface or pull off paint when it's removed.

### Repositionable Adhesive Sprays

For holding stencils, adhesive sprays have one big advantage over tape. The spray will hold down *all* the parts of the stencil, not just the outside edges, thus it will do a better job of keeping paint from seeping under detailed sections in the middle of the stencil. This is especially helpful when you're stenciling on a smooth, slick surface.

When you're buying a can of adhesive spray, make sure you see one word on it—*repositionable*! If you don't, you may be permanently attaching a stencil to your surface. Some adhesive sprays can be used for a variety of artistic and craft tasks; others are specifically stencil adhesives. Either is fine to use as long as the label says the adhesive is repositionable and can be used with the materials—plastic, paper, fabric, or whatever—that your stencil and surface are made of.

Always apply chemical sprays in a well-ventilated area. Lightly spray the back of the stencil—it's not supposed to stick forever, you know—and let it dry

before using. You can remove spots of adhesive from hard surfaces or paper with a soft art eraser.

### Liquid Stencil Adhesives

Another option for securing stencils is to use a liquid stencil adhesive. These usually come in a bottle with a sponge applicator. Dab the sponge applicator to the smooth side of the stencil, and use rubbing alcohol to remove any excess.

## ...to Make Your Mark

Yes, you'll want to get some brushes to stencil with. But you can also use just about anything to apply paint. Cotton balls and swabs, sponges, old rags, cheesecloth, foam rubber—take a look around your house and add to the list. Each different applicator you use will produce its own texture and color. Sponges, for example, will give a less filled-in, more mottled look.

### Stenciling Brushes

A stencil brush has short, firmly packed bristles. You can find them in various widths, from tiny ones for detail work to large ones for painting large sections. Typical sizes range from less than ¼ inch to 2 inches (6 mm to 5.1 cm) in diameter. The advantage of those stiff bristles, as compared to those on a normal paintbrush, is that they make it easier to keep the paint within the area you intend it for, and not under the stencil's edges.

Most stencil brushes have either natural or nylon bristles. Natural bristles are generally a better bet (naturally) as they absorb paint well and have a good combination of being relatively flexible but stiff enough when necessary. Nylon bristles tend to be much stiffer, making them better suited for painting with the stippling method (more on that later).

Stencil brushes are available *flat tipped* or *domed*. The bristles of flat-tipped brushes are all one length. Domed brushes have bristles that are slightly tapered near the ends to form the shape of, well, you know. Either kind of brush will do, though domed brushes are better for producing shaded effects.

Keep several brushes on hand, using the same one for each color employed in a project. If you simply rinse

### BEHIND THE MASK

Besides holding stencils down, masking tape can live up to its name by masking certain parts of the stencil as you paint other parts. In this way, a single overlay stencil can achieve the more complex effects of a multiple overlay. Just cover part of the stencil with tape and paint the rest with one color. Then reposition the tape and switch to another color.

out a yellow brush, for example, and then dip it into blue paint, you will make the blue paint too watery. (And, if you didn't rinse out the brush thoroughly enough, you may rediscover that yellow + blue = green.)

## Sponge or Foam Brushes

You can also go beyond the bristle and choose a foam or sponge brush for stenciling. They're easy to use and produce a different texture from regular brushes. If you're using a thicker paint, you may want to dilute it with a little water to keep the pores of the sponge from clogging.

## FIT TO SIZE

Here's a good rule of thumb (or rule of brush): Your stenciling brush should be about half the size of the area to be painted. This means you shouldn't use a tiny brush to cover a large area, or try to fill in small details with a too-wide brush. After all, you wouldn't paint a wall with a fine artist's brush, and Rembrandt (we have to assume) wouldn't work on a portrait with a paint roller.

## Foam Rollers

For covering larger areas with a single color, high-density foam rollers are a great choice. Foam rollers are designed to apply less paint—they don't hold as much paint as traditional nap rollers (the kind you'd use to paint the ceiling). When your stenciling expertise has progressed from decorating a small pillow to covering a large wall, foam rollers are the way to go.

## Other Applicators

**Artist's brushes**—You can be just like Van Gogh (sort of) and use small, thin artist's brushes to add details like shadows or leaf veins.

**Paint pens**—When precision is a must, or you need to touch up a smudge or scratch, consider using a paint pen or paint marker. You can find paint pens to use on a variety of surfaces, from metal to fabric.

**Small plastic squeeze bottles with very small tips**—These paint applicators allow you to outline motifs with a fine line, add detail, or write words.

**Finely textured makeup sponges**—These work well for applying paint to glass or tile.

## ...to Color Your World

All paints have one thing in common: They're made up of a pigment, a binder, and a solvent. Beyond that, each type of paint comes with its own advantages and disadvantages.

When you're standing in the craft, art supply, or hardware store aisle, follow one piece of advice: Read the label! Every paint container has instructions on how to use the paint, what surfaces you can put it on, drying time, cleanup, and more. If you have the time, practice using the paint you buy on the type of surface you've chosen for your project.

### Acrylic Paints

These water-based paints are long-lasting, resilient, and adhere well. They dry fast, have little smell, and clean up with water. The acrylic paints you find in plastic bottles or glass jars have a smooth, creamy consistency. Those paints you find in tubes (the kind artists more often use) have a thicker, buttery texture—not quite like toothpaste but headed there. The "hobby" type paints sold in plastic bottles are of varying quality, and usually have a lesser load of pigment than the artist varieties in tubes.

Acrylic paint can be very liquid, making it easy to get too much paint on the brush and allow it to seep under the stencil. To keep brushes workable while stenciling with them, you may need to load them with gel-blending medium and work them on paper towels to clean and soften.

One upside of the quick drying time of acrylic paints is that they don't smudge as easily as some other paints. Once cured, acrylic paint is irreversible and water insoluble; you can remove it with denatured alcohol, lacquer thinner, or acetone.

### Latex Paints

Let's say you're stenciling a field of poppies all the way around your apartment. You'd need a boatload of those little acrylic paint tubes to make it to the end, wouldn't you? Instead, head to the home-improvement store and peruse your choices of latex paints. These paints are water-based, nontoxic, inexpensive, and easy to clean up. They work best on hard surfaces like walls and furniture.

Latex paints dry slowly and smudge easily, so work carefully with them if you're not very experienced at stenciling. Latex paint dries quickly to the touch (it feels dry when the water has evaporated), but it hasn't cured until the solvent has evaporated.

### Oil Paints

If latex paints are slow to dry, oil paints are even slower. This means they smudge very easily, but the longer drying time makes them ideal for blending and creating smudgy shadows. They're also less likely to run under the stencil than latex paint. Cleaning up is more difficult with oil paints, though, as they require mineral spirits or brush cleaner.

You can apply oil paint to many surfaces, including walls, paper, fabric, and wood. Oil is the best choice if you need to stencil on a surface that has an oil paint base coat. Be as careful as possible with oil paints; if you do make any smudges, you can do touch-ups with a white art gum eraser.

### Stencil Creams

Stencil cream (or crème) has a thick, creamy consistency like lipstick or shoe polish. It won't run, drip, or seep under stencil edges. Stencil creams contain a small amount of oil, but they clean up easily with soap and water. As with oil paints, you can blend them easily to create soft, smooth, translucent colors. They also work well on fabrics and stay soft to the touch when dry.

Stencil cream typically comes in a jar. It's self-sealing, meaning that a thin, protective film of dry paint will form over the top of the paint after it is used. You can remove this film with a paper towel.

## Stencil Crayons

These oil-based paints come in stick form and are made especially for stenciling. To use them, break the seal by rubbing the stick onto your stencil or other surface, then rub your brush into that corner, working the paint into the bristles. Different types are available, from easy to blend to slow to dry. They are similar to stencil creams.

## Spray Paint

Spray paint is quick to use, gives a flat, even finish, and is great for larger projects—as long as you can ensure that the paint will not produce an "overspray" that drifts into areas outside the stencil. You'll also need to work outdoors or in a space with very good ventilation. You should wear a painter's mask and gloves while using spray paints because spray paint is toxic when wet. It's better to use two fine coats of spray paint than one thick, gloppy one. Traditionally enamel-based, spray paints now come in acrylic water-based varieties, which are less flammable, have less of an odor, and clean up with soap and water.

## Fabric Paints & Dyes

You can use a variety of paints on fabric. Artist and hobby acrylics, for example, adhere well to most fabrics, though they get a little stiff when dry. To help the paint saturate the cloth fibers, you can mix acrylic paints with flow enhancers or fabric medium. This also helps the fabric remain soft after the paint has dried—an essential for baby clothes or anything worn next to the skin. Stenciled fabric that is not to be worn—such as curtains, pillows, placemats, and other home decoration items—can be a little stiffer.

Products sold specifically as fabric paints are designed to adhere strongly enough to make it through a washing, while remaining pliable enough to keep the cloth soft. Textile paints, specifically designed to be both washable and dry-cleanable, may need to dry for 24 hours and be heat set.

Fabric paints form a coating on the surface of the cloth. Fabric dyes, on the other hand, form molecular bonds with the fiber itself. Most dyes are so fluid that they don't really work for stenciling unless combined with a thickener such as sodium alginate. You can use fabric dyes to create a background color to serve as the canvas (perhaps literally, depending on your choice of fabric) for your stenciling designs.

## Paint Mediums

A medium is not a paint itself. It's something you add to a paint to change its qualities. A gloss medium, for example, increases a paint's sheen and enhances the color depth, while a matte medium decreases the sheen. Other mediums for acrylic paint include airbrush mediums and thickeners, iridescent, opaque, or transparent mediums, and textural mediums. A bottle of textile medium can turn your collection of ordinary acrylic paints into fabric paints. Just add textile medium to your acrylic paints in equal parts.

## Special Effects Paints

When you replace or enhance some of the standard pigments in paints with things like mica flakes, dyes, or metal, you end up with these special effects paints. Best of all, your stenciled project ends up with a lot of sparkle, shine, glow, and pizazz.

**Dimensional paints**—These paints, often made for use on fabrics, come in squeeze bottles in an array of colors. They're water-based, nontoxic, and usually machine-washable.

**Iridescent paints**—Add titanium-coated mica flakes with an outer layer of a transparent light-absorbing colorant to paint, and what you get—besides a really long mouthful to say—are these sparkly paints. Also known as metallic paints, they do not tarnish and can be used to create an appearance similar to that of bronzing powders.

**Interference paints**—These colorless, transparent paints also include titanium-coated mica flakes (which, if you think about it, sound like a kind of cereal only robots would eat). They are also known as *opalescent colors*, and they change color depending upon the angle at which you view them. Light either hits the mica flakes directly, reflecting the labeled

# "Green" Paint

Today, you can find a variety of safe, non-toxic, and environmentally friendly paints to use in your stencil projects. Many interior home paint manufacturers are developing "green" paints. Look for products that are free of volatile organic compounds (VOCs), which are a large group of carbon-based chemicals that have been linked to numerous health issues, including eye, nose, and throat irritation, nausea, headaches, and even cancer. These products are only a bit more expensive than regular paint. If you don't want to buy a whole can of interior paint for one small stencil project, keep in mind that some manufacturers sell sample jars of paint that are small and inexpensive. You'll save on wasted paint and wasted money.

Also worth checking out are "milk-based" paints, which are made from milk protein, lime, and earth or mineral pigments. Although these emit no chemicals, they should not be used in damp areas, like kitchens or bathrooms. Milk-based paints also take a long time to dry and require frequent repainting.

You can find paints made with other natural materials as well, such as linseed, citrus, and soy oils, pine- and balsam-derived turpenes, minerals, plant pigments, lime, and chalk.

For acrylic paints and other small-scale art supplies, look for the "AP" seal given by the Art & Creative Materials Institute, Inc., which evaluates the toxicity of art supplies. The AP seal is found on products that contain "no materials in sufficient quantities to be toxic or injurious to humans or to cause acute or chronic health problems."

color, or passes to another layer that displays a complementary color. The effect is like that of thin coat of oil floating on water.

**Fluorescent paints**—These intense, brilliant colors have the neat trick of reflecting more visible light than they receive. They absorb invisible ultraviolet light and give off visible light of a longer wavelength. The fluorescent effect, as well as the color, fades fairly soon, so these paints are not a good choice for stenciled works that are intended to last.

**Metallic powders**—These are not paints, but fine powders you apply to an almost dry coat of varnish. They give your project an embossed gilt look. You need a well-prepared surface to use metallic powders, and it can be difficult to place the powder exactly where you want to. Practice using them before embarking on a big project.

## Finishes

Finishes aren't paints either, but they are sometimes essential for sealing and protecting your carefully stenciled creation. They can also change the sheen of your project or give greater depth to colors. Finish coats should be applied to anything that will be walked on, like a floorcloth, and it's a good idea to apply them to most furniture. Finishes include shellac, varnish, and water-based finishes like acrylic varnish.

When applying a finish, work in an well-ventilated area and thoroughly dust the surface before beginning. Use several thin coats instead of one or two heavy ones. Clear coats range from matte to gloss, and you can also choose between brush-on or spray finishes.

# ...to Complete Your Toolbox

You'll find the following tools, art supplies, and house-hold items very helpful.

**Palette tray**—A flat plastic surface with a slightly raised edge to hold the paint in. You can use one for roller stenciling, mixing paint colors, or working paints into stencil brushes. Make one yourself by lining an old cookie sheet with freezer paper.

**Palette knife or putty knife**—Use one of these to blend colors on a palette or remove excess paint when roller stenciling.

**Plastic misting bottle filled with water**—Keep one of these on hand to prevent paints and stencil rollers from drying out.

**Index cards**—These small, sturdy pieces of paper are good for masking parts of the stencil you don't want to paint yet. You can also use them to cover and protect parts of the surface you're stenciling on.

**Pencil**—Use a pencil, not a pen, for marking level lines and registration marks when stenciling; the marks will be easy to erase or painted over.

**Tape measure or ruler**—Depending on the size of your project, one of these can help you determine the proper spacing for evenly aligning your stencil design.

**Level**—If you're applying a stencil to a wall or a piece of furniture, this tool helps keep designs straight.

**Art gum eraser**—This is a useful item for wiping out minor smudges when you're working with paints that dry slowly, such as stencil creams or oil paints.

**Paper towels**—With any art project—or any project at all—it's a smart idea to have paper towels on hand. Use them to wipe excess paint from brushes, protect surfaces, and clean up when you're done.

# Surface Matters

With the right paint and the right surface preparation, you can stencil on just about everything. Pick out your desired surface, prepare it as advised below, get the right paint (read those labels!), and you're ready to go.

## Wood

To get a smooth surface for stenciling, first fill any holes or cracks with wood filler. Sand the wood with 220-grit sandpaper and wipe away the dust with a tack cloth or lint-free towel. (Rough wood surfaces will work too, but the stenciled images will look less precise.) Prime the surface of the wood and/or paint a background color if you wish. Just make sure the surface is clean and dry before starting to stencil.

## Walls

As with any painting job, you have to prepare the wall surface first. As mentioned above, a smooth surface means a sharper design. Repair any cracks, holes, or other damaged areas, then cover the wall with a fresh coat of latex or oil-based paint. Latex is usually a better choice because it's quicker and easier to clean up. Flat paint is also a better idea than semigloss, as stencil paints adhere more easily to flat paint, and stencil designs will stand out better against it. If you find your stencil paint doesn't stick well to your base coat, lightly sand the area you will be stenciling next.

## HOLD STILL
Cloth—unlike, say, a wall—will move around as you apply the paint. To keep it flat, spray a little low-tack adhesive onto the work surface. Let it dry well. Spread out the cloth on the surface, smoothing any wrinkles. Be sure to test the adhesive first to see that it doesn't remain on the cloth.

## Textured Walls & Paneling

Even after reading about the virtues of flat surfaces, you might decide to stencil on a textured wall. Well, okay. If you do, know that slightly textured surfaces (such as those called "orange peel") will take a stencil better than heavily textured ones (such as "popcorn"). Choose a more open design with larger blocks of color, and not one with tiny designs. Stencil creams also may work better than acrylic paints.

If a textured wall wasn't enough of a challenge, you can also try to stencil paneling. First, wash the paneling to remove wax or dirt. If your paneling is fairly glossy, coat it with a bonder or primer followed by a coat or two of latex paint before stenciling.

## Textiles

Plain cotton fabric is easy and comfortable to work with in most situations, and that includes stenciling. Cotton gives you a smooth surface that absorbs just enough to make the paint easy to control. Cotton fabrics come in different weights and weaves; canvas, for example, is basically a heavy cotton that is very absorbent and not prone to bleeds.

Cellulose fibers—such as rayon, linen, and hemp—share many of the stenciling qualities of cotton. Evaluate synthetic fibers individually. It's a good idea to test out your stencil paint on synthetic fibers before beginning to stencil. Silk has different characteristics and can work well with dyes and paints especially made for it. Whatever fabrics you choose, prewash them and press them flat before starting to stencil.

## Paper

Paper is a great surface for practicing stenciling, but paper surfaces are not as sturdy as walls, wood, canvas, or glass. They are not sealed, and when covered with water-based paint, they can stretch or curl or even fall apart. But if you're careful, you can stencil even on materials as thin as tissue paper. You may want to use inks or pigment dyes to stencil on paper because they are drier and won't soak in as much. When using paint, try painting a base coat to stabilize the surface.

## Glass & Ceramics

It's great to be alive today. Not only can you talk on
your cell phone to anyone anywhere at anytime, but
paint-industry chemists have been working hard to
create new paints that now make it easy to stencil on
glass and ceramics. Be sure to choose paint specifically meant for glass and tile. These paints are available in transparent colors, to give a stained-glass look,
and also in opaque shades.

Paint for glass and glazed ceramics comes in two
varieties: those that will air-dry to final hardness and
those that require baking in the oven to cure. Be sure
to read and follow any manufacturer's directions.

## Metal

Be sure to use a paint that adheres well to metal. Look
for paints that don't require priming. Most likely, however, you are going to have to prime the surface first.

OH, THE PLACES THEY'LL GO!
As far as surfaces go, wood, walls,
glass, ceramics, textiles, and paper
are the very tip of the stenciling
iceberg. After a while, you might
discover that anything and everything looks better with a stencil.
Personal stencils make your things
easier to identify. Ever felt anxious
when 40 identical black roller bags
came down the chute at baggage
claim? Not anymore, now that yours
has a sparkling silver spaceship
stenciled on the front. How about
a row of perky poppies stenciled
on your laptop to make the workday just a bit more fun? Do we
even need to mention adding our
handsome skull (page 86) to your
Halloween pumpkin?

# Techniques

The stencil techniques you'll learn below are as easy as one, two, three. One: Cut out your stencils or (even easier) select one of the great ones in this book. Two: Affix your stencil to a surface. Three: Paint your stencil. When you get to step four—admire your creation and collect compliments—you won't need any special instructions.

## Cutting Your Own Stencil

Making your own stencils takes a little time and patience, but it's easy and fun. If you create the design yourself, you'll really be adding your own personal touch.

### How To: Cut a Transparent Stencil

**What You Need**

Printout of the stencil design (you can enlarge or reduce this on a photocopier)

Acetate or stiff plastic (see-through works best)

Tape (use repositionable or low-tack varieties so your stencil doesn't get sticky)

Cutting surface, such as a self-healing cutting mat, plate of tempered glass, or a piece of thick cardboard (be careful not to cut through to your tabletop!)

Craft knife with a very sharp blade

**What You Do**

**1.** Secure the printout of the stencil design to the piece of acetate with a few pieces of tape along the edges so that it doesn't slip as you cut. Make sure to leave a border of acetate at least an inch (2.5 cm) around the whole design.

**2.** On your cutting surface, use your craft knife to carefully cut out the stencil, following the lines of the original.

**3.** Once you've cut out the whole design, tidy up any rough edges. If you make a mistake—such as cutting through a connective bridge in your design (oops!)— you can repair it with a small piece of masking tape (see Nobody's Perfect, page 27).

### How To: Cut an Opaque Stencil

**What You Need**

Same as for a transparent stencil, only your stencil material isn't transparent (naturally), and you need a spray adhesive instead of tape

**What You Do**

**1.** Spray the back of a paper pattern with stencil adhesive. (See How To: Use Spray Adhesive, page 19.) Stick the pattern onto a sheet of stencil material, such as cardboard, opaque plastic, or freezer paper.

**2.** Working on your cutting surface, carefully cut along the pattern lines with a craft knife, cutting through both the stencil and the pattern.

**3.** Peel off the pattern.

## STENCIL SMARTS: CUTTING OUT STENCILS

- You'll control the knife better and be able to apply pressure more evenly if you always cut toward yourself.

- How do you make sure you always cut toward yourself? Just rotate your work as you go so it is always in the right position and you're cutting at a comfortable angle.

- You can use your free hand to hold the acetate and stencil more firmly on the cutting board—just keep your fingers away from that sharp blade!

- Press firmly so you cut all the way through the stencil on one pass.

- For curving sections, try to make long cuts without lifting the cutting tool so that you'll produce a smooth curve with no breaks.

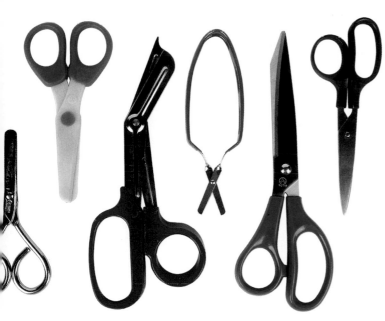

## How To: Cut a Stencil with a Heat Cutter

I mentioned using heat cutters for stencils back in the Things You'll Need… section. They look like little soldering irons and—like soldering irons—they get really, really hot. If you keep their points sharp and work with care, you'll find them easier to use than craft knives. If you don't work with care, you'll find I wasn't kidding when I said they are really, really hot.

### What You Need
Heat cutter

The same materials you used for a transparent stencil—only don't use a cutting mat, as the heat would damage it. (And don't use a craft knife, as you have this nifty heat cutter to try out.)

### What You Do
**1.** Preheat the heat cutter. Tape the acetate or plastic on top of the pattern.

**2.** Place the stencil material and pattern on top of a piece of safety glass or thick cardboard.

**3.** Hold the heat cutter like a pencil and trace along the lines of the pattern with its tip. The heat will melt a line in the film, so you must keep the tip moving at a steady rate to give the line an even width. He who hesitates is not exactly lost, but he has made a big hole in the film.

## Adhering a Stencil to a Surface

In creating stencils, you may use tape or spray adhesive to attach the stencil material to the pattern. Now that you have a stencil (yay!), you use one of those methods for affixing the stencil to the surface to be painted. Here's some advice on doing it the spray way.

### How To: Use Spray Adhesive
**What You Need**
Spray adhesive (make sure it's not permanently bonding!)

Stencil and surface to be stenciled

**What You Do**
**1.** Read the manufacturer's instructions and follow all safety guidelines.

**2.** Hold the can about 8 inches (20.3 cm) from the back of the stencil and spray enough to cover most of the stencil sheet.

**3.** Allow the spray to set up (as per directions on can) and dry on the stencil before sticking to the surface.

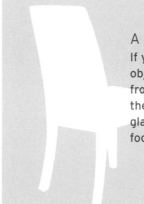

### A TRANSPARENT SOLUTION
If you're stenciling any glass objects people might eat or drink from, be sure to paint underneath the plate or on the outside of the glasses rather than on surfaces food will come in contact with.

# Stenciling with Paint

There are two very popular tried-and-true methods for stenciling with paint: *stippling* (also known as *pouncing*) and *swirling*. To stipple—the word just sounds fun, doesn't it?—you tap or dab the loaded brush against the stencil openings. This method creates more even tones and less depth. For swirling, make simple circular brush motions against the stencil openings.

## How To: Apply Paint with a Brush

### What You Need
Paint

Palette tray or plate

Stencil brush

### What You Do

**1.** Put a dollop of paint onto a palette tray or plate. Pick up a small amount of paint on the end of a clean stencil brush. On a clean part of the palette or plate, work the paint thoroughly into the ends of the bristles by rubbing the brush in firm circles.

**2.** Work the brush in circles on a stack of paper towels to off-load any excess paint.

**3.** You can either stipple (pounce) or swirl the paint onto the surface. Either way, hold the brush straight up and down. To stipple, pounce the brush over the stencil cutouts with short, hard taps. To swirl, rub it in small circles over the cutouts, lightly at first and then more firmly.

**4.** When you have filled in the cutouts to your liking, carefully remove the stencil.

## STENCIL SMARTS: APPLYING THE PAINT

- You can use the fingers of your free hand to hold down small parts of the stencil as you apply the paint.

- For darker color, put down a light coat and cover it with one or more coats. Putting down just one heavy coat of paint could result in a sloppy stencil.

- Go ahead and lift a corner of the stencil to check your work, but don't pick it up entirely until you are done. It is very difficult to put it back in the same spot.

## How To: Stencil with Spray Paint

**What You Need**
Paper and tape for masking the nearby area

Spray paint

**What You Do**
**1.** Mask off an area around the stencil with paper and tape. If you're stenciling on a wall, protect the floor with newspaper or a drop cloth.

**2.** Hold the can about 8 to 10 inches (20.3 to 25.4 cm) away from the surface. Start spraying into the masked area, off the stencil opening, and then slowly and evenly move the spray over the stencil. Keep the spray moving in a sweeping motion, and use light coats of paint.

**3.** Gradually build up the color. It's better to apply too little than too much.

**4.** Lift the stencil carefully. Wet paint on the stencil can cause smudges.

## How To: Apply Paint with a Roller

**What You Need**
Paint

Palette tray or lined cookie sheet

Palette knife

High-density foam roller

Paper towels

**What You Do**
**1.** Pour a small amount of paint onto a palette tray or a cookie sheet lined with freezer paper. With a palette knife, streak the puddle until it is long, wide, and shallow.

**2.** Roll a dry foam roller through the paint streak, moving it back and forth until it is covered evenly.

**3.** To off-load, run the roller on a stack of paper towels.

**4.** Draw the roller across the stencil openings. Press lightly at first and then a bit harder. Keep the roller flat to avoid building up paint in any edges.

**5.** Carefully remove the stencil.

### A LITTLE DAB WILL DO YA
When stenciling, you should use the least amount of paint possible. Before your brush or roller leaves the jar or tray, make sure you "off-load" (a fancy word for "remove") all excess paint. Paint tends to creep or bleed under the edges of the stencil, so you want to make sure you're using the absolute minimum needed. You'll have to dip your brush into the paint more often, but the clean lines of your end result will be worth it.

## Stenciling on Fabric

Yes, there are some differences between textiles and solid surfaces like walls and furniture. Many painting techniques are no different, however, when you change your stencil surface from shelves to shirts. The following tips cover those techniques that don't remain the same.

• Wash and dry your new fabric according to the label instructions to remove the sizing (chemical coating) it has. If you don't, the paint won't bond properly.

• Place a piece of cardboard between the layer of fabric being stenciled and the one below. Paint can bleed through fabric, and you don't want to stencil the front of your shirt and the inside of the back at the same time.

• Paint soaks straight into fabric, so you may need to use more of it than you would on a solid surface.

• Follow the directions for drying found on your fabric paints or stencil creams. Some paints need as long as two weeks to cure. Others may require heat from a clothes dryer or an iron.

### LIFE'S A BLEACH

Remember reverse stencils? Those are the ones where the stenciled image is really the background, leaving the design in the original color. One cool fabric technique is like that (sort of) in that you're doing the reverse of a normal stencil. It's called discharge dyeing, a technique that creates designs by removing color rather than adding it.

Here's how it's done: You apply bleach to the fabric over the stencil area, and the original fabric dyes discharge. This works best with dark fabrics and natural fiber; however, it's impossible to know for sure what the final color will turn out to be. You can finely spray liquid bleach, slightly diluted, with a mister. To use a brush or roller, make a bleach paste with sodium alginate. Put a few spoonfuls of sodium alginate in a small container, then slowly add household bleach, stirring it until it is thick enough to paint with.

BIG GIANT SAFETY WARNING: Bleach is a caustic solution that can burn your skin, lungs, and eyes, so always use bleach in a well-ventilated area, and always wear protective gloves, a vapor mask, and safety goggles.

# Stenciling Glass with Etching Cream

In the same way you can remove fabric dye to produce an image on cloth (see Life's a Bleach sidebar, page 22), you can remove a little of the surface of glass to create an image. With this technique, an etching cream and a stencil combine to leave an image with an evenly frosted finish. Give it a try!

## How To: Etch Glass

### What You Need
Glass or mirror

Alcohol, vinegar, or soap

Paper towel or lint-free cloth

Stencil (ones made of self-adhesive vinyl, like contact paper, work best)

Spray adhesive

Etching cream

Spatula

### What You Do
**1.** Clean the glass or mirror with the alcohol, vinegar, or soapy water. Rinse thoroughly and dry with a paper towel or lint-free cloth.

**2.** Adhere the stencil to the glass. If you don't have a self-adhesive stencil, use spray adhesive to prevent bleeding under the stencil.

**3.** Scoop out some etching cream and spread it over the stencil openings. Let the cream sit as manufacturer's instructions recommend.

**4.** Remove most of the cream with a spatula and return it to the jar.

**5.** Keep the stencil in place and flood the surface with water to remove any remaining cream.

**6.** Remove the stencil and rinse again.

# Color & Design

A good stencil design doesn't need any fancy-pants painting techniques or intricate arrangements to make it look terrific. But if you're feeling frisky, here are a few very simple ways you can use paint and layout for extra credit.

## Get Shady

Flat, solid colors can sometimes be bold and other times a little boring. Adding some simple shading can change things up. Start working the paint more strongly on the outside edges of the opening, lightening up as you work into the center. Your design will have a darker edge and lighter center, giving depth and dimension to your stencil.

When you're shading your stencil, keep this art school tip in mind: Areas with deeper color look as though they are receding or farther away. Lighter colors bring the area into the foreground.

## Mix It Up

Just as you don't have to stick to one shade, you don't have to stick to just one color. When blending colors through a stencil, stippling rather than swirling is the way to go, as swirling can overmix the colors and muddy them. You can also blend colors using rollers. Simply roll one over another. Decorative painters use all sorts of techniques and tools to make surfaces resemble stone, tile, wood, and more. Try some of them with a stencil, and impress people both with your surface and your design.

## Superimpose Patterns

How do you make a flat surface look textured? Just layer a thin sheet of screen-like material with a stencil. You can combine your stencil with manufactured materials like cheesecloth, lace, window screens, or whatever else you can think of. (This is a good time to try out your technique on a test surface, not on your favorite end table.) Tape the patterned material in place on the stencil to keep it steady.

## Freehanding

Did you have trouble staying within the lines of your coloring books as a kid? (I know I did.) Stencils are made to help you re-create a design, but you're not legally required to stay inside the precut curves, you know. Add some hand-painted details, and you'll both add interest to your piece and make it a unique, personally created object. Outlining a stenciled print makes it a bolder statement—and can cover up edges that weren't quite as sharp as you'd hoped.

When you're thinking outside the stencil, you can also think outside your same old stencil brushes. Apply details with whatever art materials you'd like. Paint pens look like felt-tip pens, but contain water-based paint. You can use a fine-tipped squeeze bottle filled with paint to give a raised effect to your personal touch.

## Freestyling

I'm not talking about turning up a beat and rapping as you stencil—though go ahead and try that if you want to. (Whatever unlocks your creativity is a good thing, though possibly not for your roommate or close neighbors.) This kind of freestyle means that you can group and arrange stencils however you like to make your own compositions. You want to overlap designs or make them in a variety of sizes? Go for it! You can use different motifs in the same project as well. Others may not have seen the connection between a bumble-bee stencil and a skull design before, but they will once you put them together. Whether they'll like them together is another question, but you should feel free to at least consider whether it works for you.

## Off the Wall

Before you picked up this book and flipped through its unexpected designs, what is the first thing you would you have thought if someone had suddenly barked "Stencil!" at you? (After "That guy must be crazy," that is.) You probably would have pictured a repeating decorative border around the ceiling of a room, either in a Greco-Roman architectural motif, a still life of grapevines, or with some frolicking woodland creatures.

Well, just because room borders have been done so much doesn't mean you can't do them too. A couple of things to keep in mind: One, you're not limited to traditional-looking borders, now that you have the fresh designs included in this book and the ability to make designs of your own choosing. And two, you can do more than just circle around the ceiling. Border designs offer great ways to accent windows, doors, panels, screens, frames, furniture, or even stationery.

When you're making any linear stencil motif, you have to plan how to keep the repeated design level and in position. Making guidelines and using registration marks to transition from one stencil application to the next is essential. You'll also have to keep an eye out for corners—both the ones you might run into going around the walls of a room and the ones in any rectangular frame. Try to stop or start at corners in a way that won't disrupt your pattern.

## Beyond Paint

The materials you can use to stencil an image are limitless. In researching this book, I've run across tightly coiffed "up-dos" enhanced with a stencil. The hair stylist used temporary (and glittery!) hair color to create something very special. I've seen sunblock applied through a stencil so that a suntan becomes a work of art. OK, so you don't have to take the idea to such extremes. As an example, see our Jack Frosting cupcakes (page 94), which have a stenciled frosting design that looks fabulous for the short time they aren't eaten.

## Aging Gracefully

Sometimes it's good to be distressed. Give your stenciled project timeworn character by distressing the surface with color washes or glazes or by using a special crackled paint. Roughing up the surface or edges with sandpaper can also be effective. Make your stencils harken back to a golden age with the opulent effects of metal, foil, leaf, or powders.

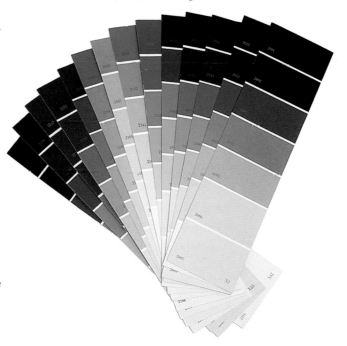

# Clean Up

A great cook probably isn't too excited about thoroughly washing the saucepans after preparing a delicious meal, but she will be sorry the next day if she doesn't. In the same way, once you do a great job on that gorgeous stenciling project, you need to do an equally great job of cleaning your paint palette, stencils, and brushes. Carefully cleaning and drying your tools means you'll be able to use them for a long time. Yes, I know this part of the stenciling process is totally boring, but it's also entirely necessary. Sorry! The following advice and tips should help.

## Stencils

Cleaning stencils is a lot easier if you don't let them sit for a long time covered with dried stencil paint. How you clean a stencil depends on the paint you're using and the material the stencil is made from. With acrylic paint and a typical plastic (such as polyester film) stencil, try soaking the stencil in warm, soapy water. You can also wipe it with a baby wipe or with nail polish remover (the acetone type). For stencil creams, wiping with a paper towel or other soft cloth should be enough. To remove adhesive from the backs of stencils, mineral spirits work well.

## Stencil Brushes

Brushes with acrylic or latex paint should clean up easily with mild soap (like dishwashing liquid) and water followed by a thorough rinsing. If they don't, you might be using too much paint on your brush—a lesson to learn for next time! If you're using stencil creams, you may need rubbing alcohol followed by mineral spirits. Oil-based paints in general require paint thinner or mineral spirits to clean. Whatever kind of paint or cleaner you use, don't soak the brushes in them overnight. Finish the cleanup job as soon as you can.

## Foam Rollers

Unlike those nappy paint rollers you paint the ceiling with and toss out, foam rollers for stenciling can and should be cleaned. Wet the roller thoroughly, then work soap and water through the foam with your hands. Squeeze the water out, wet it again, and squeeze again (rinse and repeat) until the water runs clear. Pull the foam head off the handle and allow both parts to dry.

## STENCIL SMARTS: TIPS AND TRICKS

- Practice makes perfect—or at least it makes your first try better and more confident. Try out new techniques and designs on paper first, then you can adjust as needed when it comes to painting the real thing.

- If your masking tape is stickier than you need (and you don't have any painter's tape on hand), make the tape a little less sticky by sticking it to your shirt or other cloth before using it on the stencil.

- Stenciling is always fun, but it can get tiring. Make sure that you place the piece you're stenciling on a table or counter where you can work on it at a comfortable height and position. If you're working on a wall (something a little harder to move), use a stool or ladder to get to the right position to stencil without strain.

- Take a break when you need to! Just stand back and admire your developing handiwork for a while, rather than pushing on to the point where you're more likely to make mistakes.

- Store your stencils flat in boxes or drawers. Large stencils can be hung on pants hangers in your closet—just make sure you've cleaned off all the wet paint first!

# Nobody's Perfect

Two common problems you'll find when stenciling are too much paint on the brush and a stencil that shifts in the middle of painting with it. The result can be an image that is blotchy and blurry—not at all perfect. Here are some simple remedies for avoiding and correcting those problems and a few more.

## Seepage

If paint is seeping behind the stencil, you're probably using too much. With just a little seepage, you can touch up and smooth out the blurred area with an artist's brush. (Hey, nobody's going to know the stencil opening didn't really go over quite that far once you put the stencil away.) If you notice the mistake immediately, you can try to carefully wipe off the excess paint with a damp cloth. If you're stenciling on a painted background you have a third possible solution: Paint over the blotched shape with background paint. If it's a really big mistake, you can paint the whole section over, let it dry, and stencil it again. This time, remember one key word: off-load!

## Shifting

Parts of your design may end up with "ghost images," which sounds kind of cool but probably isn't the look you want. This is a result of your stencil shifting as you paint because it's not secured well enough. You may need to use larger pieces of masking tape or place tape around more of the stencil. Spray adhesive lessens slippage, so you may want to switch to it if tape isn't doing the job.

## Rips & Tears

If your plastic stencil tears, you can fix it with a small piece of cellophane or clear shipping tape on the front and back of the torn section. Adhere the tape first, and then use a craft knife to trim it even with the edge of the stencil. For paper stencils, masking tape works well.

## Color Casts

If you're stenciling over a dark base color, it can make your stencil look dark as well. One way to fix this is to stencil first with an opaque white paint mixed with a little of your final color. After this coat dries, re-stencil over it with your desired color.

# Get Shopping!

You've got the techniques and advice; now it's time to go get the paint and supplies! Here are most of the things you'll need and where to get them.

| What You Need | Where to Get It | Notes |
| --- | --- | --- |
| Paints, glazes, and faux-finishing products; painter's and masking tape | Paint, hardware, and building-supply stores | For big stenciling projects like walls, larger containers can be much more economical than small bottles or tubes |
| Art and craft paints; stencil and artist's brushes | Online suppliers and stores that carry craft supplies and fine art materials | Higher quality brushes will pay off in the long run |
| Fabric paints | Craft, fabric, and quilting stores | Read the directions carefully for what fabrics to use and how to cure the paint |
| Spray adhesive | Craft and art supply stores | Three words: repositionable! repositionable! repositionable! |
| Freezer paper | Supermarkets | Available in various brand names |
| Plastic shelf liners | Hardware and home-supply stores | The kind labeled "reposition-able" has the low-tack adhesive you want |
| Overhead transparency film | Office and educational supply stores | This film is usually thinner than materials such as Mylar |
| Plastic (such as Mylar) and other transparent films | Art supply stores and plastic suppliers | Plastic is sold in sheets and rolls in various thicknesses |

# Lotus Rococo

This lovely lily gets the royal treatment in a takeoff on a more traditional damask design. Use pastels for a sweet look or meditate on the modern with bold graphics and spray paint.

## SILVER MIST SKIRT

Stencils are a great way to dress up thrift-store finds.

I painted this skirt with spray paint, which can bleed a little depending on the material. That's fine with me, because when the paint bleeds it creates a feathered and somewhat ghostly effect. You'll want to test your paint on a small piece of fabric before painting the entire skirt and wipe the stencil between applications.

**Ursula Gullow,** *designer*

29

To make the background circles, I outlined a dinner plate in pencil and filled it in with bold colors.

Take care with corners and stepped surfaces: If the design must follow a dip in the chest, gently rub paint into the dip or around a corner. If you find this difficult, paint the flat portions of the stencil first and reposition the stencil in the dips.

**Joan K. Morris,** *designer*

TREASURED CHEST

# PRETTY & PROPER

I applied white dimensional fabric paint to the silk seat using a makeup sponge, then immediately removed the stencil.

For the seat back, I used a very dry sponge and black paint.

You'll want to dab most of the paint off your dry sponge before applying it to the chair and use a light touch while painting.

**Joan K. Morris,** *designer*

*Bonus Round*
Tissue holder
Kitchen cabinets
Party napkins

31

# Borderline

Just because a stencil looks traditional doesn't mean you can't find nontraditional ways to use it. Border stencils have so many possibilities, we can't begin to list them all. Here are a few new twists on the classic.

## BEVERAGE EDGES

Using etching liquid can be very tricky. Make sure you securely adhere your stencil to the glass and proceed slowly.

Here, using only part of a stencil produces dramatic results.

**Tyler Rogero,** *designer*

Undercoating in a lighter paint color made the topcoat "pop." Try it and see for yourself.

As this clip shows, you can stencil a border on something even if it's just as wide as your design.

**Morris Shakespeare,** *designer*

# SECURING THE BORDERS

Hum-Dinger Hummus
People have been enjoying hummus snacks for thousands of years. You can taste for yourself why it hasn't gotten old yet. Scoop the hummus to your mouth with pita bread, olives, cucumber sticks, or carrot sticks.
EQUIPMENT
can opener • strainer • blender or food processor • chef's knife • cutting board • blender or food processor • rubber spatula • vegetable peeler
2 TO 4 SERVINGS
• 1 15 oz. can garbanzo beans (also called chickpeas)
• 1 clove of garlic, peeled
• 3 tablespoons tahini (You can find this sesame seed paste with international foods or peanut butter, depending on the grocery store.)
• 1 tablespoon olive oil
• salt
• 1 lemon, halved
• water (optional)
• paprika (optional)
• 2 pieces of pita bread cut into wedges (optional)
• 1 medium cucumber, peeled and cut into sticks (optional)
• 2 medium carrots, peeled and cut into sticks (optional)
1. Open the can of garbanzo beans. Strain the juice, and rinse the beans with fresh water. Put the beans into the blender.
2. Add the garlic, tahini, olive oil, and salt to the blender or food processor. Next, squeeze the juice from the lemon into the blender. (A good trick is to hold your hand over the blender, and let the juice dribble between your fingers so you catch the seeds, or you can use a strainer.)
3. Put the lid on the blender, and blend away! You're going for a smooth mush. If you need to, stop the blender, and use the rubber spatula to push the ingredients off of the sides and into the center.
4. If the mixture is too stiff, blend in a little water to thin it out.
5. Scrape the hummus with the rubber spatula into a serving dish. You can sprinkle a little paprika on top. It looks cool and tastes great.
28
finger-lickin' good

# 'ZINE QUEEN

I wanted the lines of this stencil to remain sharp and in focus, so I dabbed the paint on with a sponge brush.

If you're using acrylic paint, be careful not to mix in too much water. This can cause the color to bleed underneath your stencil, blurring the outlines.

**Cassie Moore,** *designer*

# SMART SHADE

Before you begin: Buy paint designed to be used on glass and that can stand up to the heat the bulb will produce.

Turn the lamp on and check the shade. Touch up the paint where it needs to be thicker.

**Morris Shakespeare,** *designer*

*Bonus Round*
File folders
Picture frame
Luggage tag

# A Chair Affair

Here's a stylish stencil you can use as is, reversed, or in pieces. It's the universal symbol for "taking a load off." Pull up a chair (or four) and explore the possibilities.

Bienvenue

Flan au Roquefort

Filet Mignon aux Oignons
Gratin dauphinois

Congolais

Bon appetit!

It's easy to make several variations of the same menu with a little help from a copy machine.

Creating your own menu makes a dinner party special enough. But a one-of-a-kind stenciled dinner menu? In French? Now that's really raising the bar.

**Tyler Rogero,** *designer*

With its big solid shapes, this stencil is easy to work with. Get bold and creative!

Pick two placemats in complementary colors, and then find similar colors for painting the stencil designs. Make half of your placemats each way, and you've got a great set to alternate around the table.

**Ursula Gullow,** *designer*

# SEATED DINNER

When I saw the chair motif, I knew it would make a great slipcover design. Then I remembered the butterfly chairs in my garden shed. The covers are mostly flat and in one piece, making stenciling on them a snap.

Don't be afraid to cut a stencil in half to make it fit over a bulky seam. Work with one half at a time and mask the other half with painter's tape. Allow your first stenciled portion to dry before you attempt the second.

**Terry Taylor,** *designer*

*Bonus Round*
Side table
Lap desk
Binder

# Hot Wheels

A fun design at any size, this stencil is for those on the go. Whether it decorates clothes or a lunchbox, everyone will see at a glance that you're the wheel deal.

## CRUISIN'

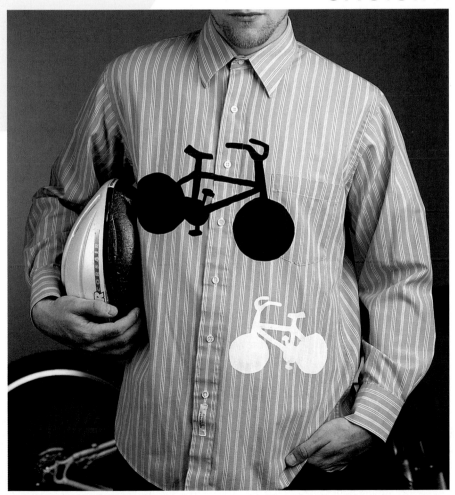

I used clear contact paper for the stencil and a piece of cardboard inside the shirt to hold the fabric flat.

Using a makeup sponge to apply fabric paint is a good idea. Be sure you use enough paint to get good coverage. Let the paint dry completely before stenciling another bicycle.

**Joan K. Morris,** *designer*

# BIKE MESSENGER

Want a grittier, street-cred vibe? Avoid the "freshly stenciled" look. To age the image on the brand-new messenger bag, I rubbed the paint with a coarse sanding sponge to reveal a bit of the bag's surface.

While sanding the entire surface of the bag, some of the stitching came apart just enough to give it a worn appearance. Now we're talking!

**Terry Taylor,** *designer*

# TEENSY IN TANDEM

When using different colors like I did, be sure to clean your stencil completely between coats.

I cut a frame out of shelf lining to surround the bicycle while stenciling. It helped protect the rest of the garment.

**Joan K. Morris,** *designer*

The Remix
This bicycle motif adorns the front of a book (as do rockets and skulls) in CosmiCovers on page 104.

*Bonus Round*
Picnic blanket
Garage wall
Toy box

# Chi-Chi Chandelier

The best thing about this chandelier
is that it's so very versatile. It hangs,
it drapes, it hugs curves. Embellish it,
use multiple colors, or just paint it as is.
Shine on!

## BUILT-IN BLING

After painting the tank top,
we secured the beaded gold
necklace in loops to mimic the
chandelier's intricate design.
The beads and chain add a 3-D
quality and enhance the tank's
glam appeal.

Try different colors and different beads to create a variety of
looks. It's all in the details.

**Segment 16,** *design collective*

# ART FOR ALL

Put your own spin on things: Change the size or use only a portion of a stencil to create whatever you envision.

This project lends a touch of class to any room, from a scholarly study to a bedroom fit for a princess.

**Melissa Lichtenwald-Thomas,** *designer*

Bonus Round
Laundry hamper
Pajamas
Ceiling

Follow the stenciler's maxim: Be patient. Let the paint dry before you overlap anything.

To match the fading paint of the table, I painted the stencil designs as partly shaded rather than solid.

**Ursula Gullow,** *designer*

44

# Portrait of a Lady

This fine form, reminiscent of a paper doll, is quite the fashion plate. Her sassy ponytail and pert pose shout, "Let's get this party started!"

## HOSTESS WITH THE MOSTEST

For an extra-special detail, stitch your stenciled paper onto the preprinted larger invitation. This technique takes just seconds on a sewing machine, but will impress your guests tenfold.

**Melissa Lichtenwald-Thomas,** *designer*

# SHADOWBOX SILHOUETTE

Enamel paint works best on a glass surface. You could also experiment with the glass etching process described on page 23.

Choose from a variety of scrapbooking papers or design your own for a unique background.

**Stephanie Brown,** *designer*

You can dry-sponge fabric paint onto a new apron you've made, or renew an older apron by covering stains with strategically placed stencils.

Remove the stencil with care so you don't tear it or get paint on the fabric. Make sure the stencil is completely dry before you reuse it.

**Joan K. Morris,** *designer*

# HIP HOMEMAKER

*Bonus Round*
Cosmetics bag
Handheld mirror
Robe

# Mayan Magic

Historical icons of an ancient people return to brighten your home. Used together or individually, these three symbols can turn your humble abode into a temple of culture.

GREAT GRAINS

I created this stencil using contact paper and spray paint.

Does one of these symbols really signify "oats" (for example) and another one "rice"? They do if you say so.

**Beth Sweet,** *designer*

PRIMITIVE LIGHT

You may need another set of hands for this project: one set to hold the stencil in place around the candle and another to apply the hot wax.

I melted old candles in a double boiler and kept the burner going at a low heat. Remember that melted wax often looks much lighter in color than it appears in candle or block form.

Wrap the stencil around the candle and dip a brush into the wax. Gently dab it onto the design. Build up the colors of the wax in thin layers, one section at a time. Before the wax completely dries, raise the stencil slowly and carefully. You may need to cut around the wax a little.

**Beth Harvey,** *designer*

# RELIC RUNNER

After positioning the stencil on the table runner, I used a makeup sponge to apply the fabric paint, dabbing it on and making sure it covered well.

If the stencil isn't sticking well enough, use a little spray adhesive on the sticky side.

**Joan K. Morris,** *designer*

*Bonus Round*
Backpack
Window box
Room divider

50

# Festooned in Feathers

Let your imagination take flight and your creativity soar. With this design, you can use one, two, or all three feathers to decorate your favorite things.

## PREPSTER BIRDHOUSE

A sponge brush is handy for painting and pouncing.

If you're putting the birdhouse out in your garden (and not on your coffee table or bookshelf), be sure to first paint the wood with a primer and then use a good-quality exterior paint for both the house and the stencil. Latex paint is easiest to work with.

**Morris Shakespeare,** *designer*

# FEATHERBED

When you paint on fabric, it's best to place a piece of paper (butcher paper, waxed paper, or even newspaper) behind the fabric before applying the paint. It's especially important when stenciling T-shirts, pillowcases, and the like. Paint can seep through fabric and stain where you don't want it to.

**Terry Taylor,** *designer*

# LIGHT AND SWEET

My inspiration for this scarf was—of course—a feather boa. To make it more interesting, I enlarged some feathers and reduced a few others.

I mixed together three different colors of fabric paint as I painted, starting with the middle color. I applied one stencil at a time so the colors could blend while they were still wet.

**Beth Harvey,** *designer*

*Bonus Round*
Cat bowl
Wainscoting
Yoga mat

# Fresh Floral

This boldly graphic floral arrangement
brightens any room . . . even your closet!
The best part is that these flowers never
need watering.

BOTANIC TEE

Pre-wash all clothing before stenciling.
This will both remove any sizing (chemical coating) and make sure the fabric has
shrunk to its final size.

When using fabric paint, make sure your
stencil brush is dry. Apply the paint in
multiple thin coats.

**Melissa Lichtenwald-Thomas,** *designer*

I cut each stencil with a heated stencil cutter. They're not very expensive, and you can find them at most craft stores.

I spray-painted the stencil entirely in yellow, and applied acrylic paint accent colors over the spray paint. Voila!

**Beth Sweet,** *designer*

FLOWER FANFARE

# VERDANT VASE

Transfer stencils to polyester film or contact paper to play with registration and negative space.

**Stephanie Brown,**
*designer*

# BLACK BLOSSOM TRAY

**Bonus Round**
Dog bed
Beach umbrella
Footstool

Do you have some special small serving bowls, plates, or teacups? Consider stenciling the tray in a color that complements your set.

Make sure your base coat is completely dry before applying your stencil.

**Melissa Lichtenwald-Thomas,** *designer*

# For the Birds

Like birds rising in flight, this design has a vertical orientation that takes the eye upwards—right up to the heart-shaped negative space at its top. Choose to stencil the pair of lovebirds, or the entire flock.

## WINGING IT

In this version of reverse stenciling, the birds and branches are left in natural wood tones, while the rest of the door is painted a solid shade.

You don't have to use the entire stencil every time, you know. The leafy ends of the branches poking into the two panels and covering the doorknob add a subtle touch.

**Beth Harvey,** *designer*

While it may take you a few applications to achieve a solid white, you may stop before you get there and enjoy the variations in transparency.

**Ursula Gullow,** *designer*

# BIRD WALKING

Many of us have socks, leg warmers, leggings, or tights in our wardrobe. With a stencil, some fabric paint, a stencil brush, and a little time, you can make these fun accents completely unique.

Stuff the leggings so the design will be the appropriate size (without looking stretched) when you wear them.

Apply several layers of paint, letting it dry between applications for opacity.

**Beth Harvey,** *designer*

The Remix
These same birds are attracted to the power lines in Creative Spark on page 78, and to the slender branches of Twig Gig on page 109.

*Bonus Round*
Windowpane
Grocery tote
Greeting card

# Bee Unique

While the butterfly haphazardly flutters from place to place, the bee buzzes straight through, intent on its mission of finding the sweetest nectar. Which one are you?

I am always looking for sweet and simple last-minute gift ideas. For this project, I was inspired by the thought of summertime's goodness. Golden honey is the natural choice to fill these etched jars, but any delicacy will do.

Glass etching can be tricky at first, but with a little practice, you'll get the hang of it. Applying more stencil adhesive than usual helps to keep the etched edges sharp and clean. Use an all-purpose spray lubricant to remove the leftover stickiness.

**Melissa Lichtenwald-Thomas,** *designer*

61

## HIVE A NICE DAY

I wanted this bee to stand out ... literally. To achieve a dimensional effect, I applied the paint with a palette knife. I worked deliberately, building up one layer at a time so the paint didn't bleed under the stencil.

I decided it would be a friendlier design if the two bees faced each other. After finishing one bee, I flipped the stencil over and painted through the other side.

Three elements come together to make the finished project: a blank linen card, a slightly smaller golden middle layer, and an even smaller piece of black card stock. I assembled the elements only after I was satisfied with my bees.

**Joan K. Morris,** *designer*

Some people have a thing for kittens or cows. For me, it's always been bees. They remind me to "bee me" and to "bee present." Having these symbols stenciled on my planner and notebook helps me keep my workday relaxed and fun.

The book surfaces were challenging to stencil. The day planner is covered in slick faux leather and the notebook's cloth covering is hardly smooth. I overcame these difficulties by using a thick, dimensional paint in a squeeze bottle with a fine tip.

**Morris Shakespeare,** *designer*

WORKER BEE

*Bonus Round*
Flowerpots
Tea mug
Garden tools

# Make It Mod

Whether you think it looks like an electrical diagram or a '60s flashback, this design makes a striking accent. It also wraps around corners and curves nicely, so you can make it as long as you like.

## FLASHY TRASH

It's great to put linear, border-like designs around column items. Doing so accentuates the column by giving it a continuous feel.

Measure twice; paint once. Use a strong stencil adhesive and oil-based paint.

**Beth Harvey,** *designer*

With a design like this one, you can really get creative with colors.

If you need to use more than one color with one stencil (without moving it), keep a roll of masking tape nearby. Blocking off parts of the stencil will keep paints from accidentally mixing.

**Stephanie Brown,** *designer*

# GROUNDBREAKING STYLE

Combining practicality and artistic expression, floor-cloths originally became popular as floor coverings in the 18th century. When I first saw this design, I immediately thought of using it in a small foyer or as an accent under a coffee table.

After sewing the edges over, coat the canvas with a layer or two of gesso. Seal the cloth with coats of a non-yellowing polyurethane.

I used a painting technique called scumbling. Apply one color at a time to the cloth with a circular motion, creating a cloudy pattern. Let it dry in between colors.

**Beth Harvey,** *designer*

*Bonus Round*
Funky dress
Futon cover
Lampshade

# Mr. Roboto

"Take me to your leader!" Is this robot a friend or foe? You decide by how you use this stencil. He looks harmless by himself, but as part of an advancing crowd he becomes a little bit scary.

## ROBOT INVASION

Take one abandoned artist canvas, and add a series of stencils in varying sizes and colors. With these simple steps, you can create a masterpiece.

Look for second-hand paintings at garage sales, charity shops, and flea markets—the kitschier the better.

**Beth Sweet,** *designer*

Using the right fabric paint is especially crucial for projects like this bag, where you're combining a slick material and an object that will get plenty of wear and tear. PB&Js never tasted so out-of-this-world!

**Tyler Rogero,** *designer*

ROBOLUNCH

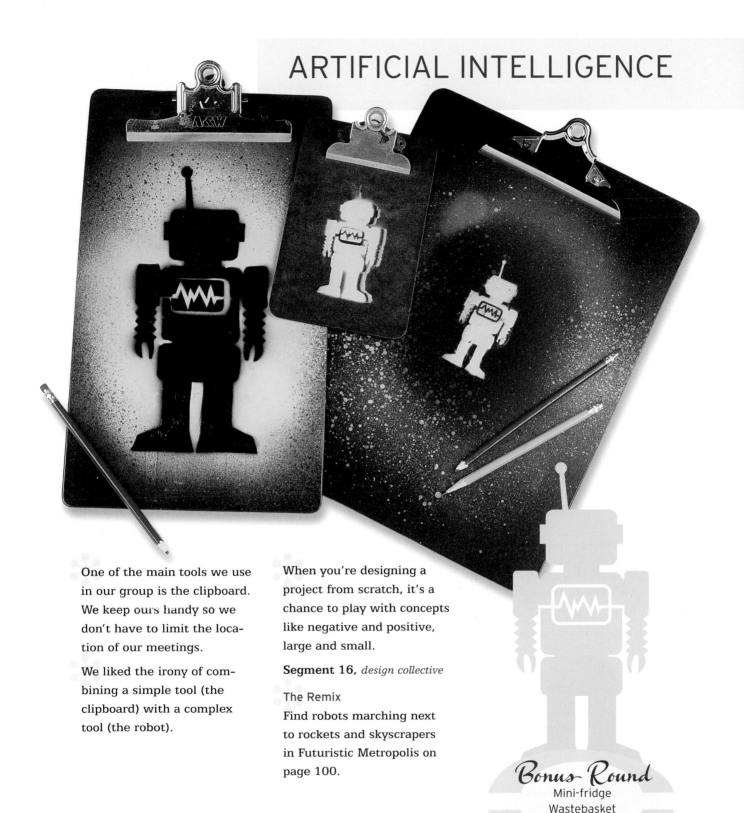

One of the main tools we use in our group is the clipboard. We keep ours handy so we don't have to limit the location of our meetings.

We liked the irony of combining a simple tool (the clipboard) with a complex tool (the robot).

When you're designing a project from scratch, it's a chance to play with concepts like negative and positive, large and small.

**Segment 16,** *design collective*

The Remix
Find robots marching next to rockets and skyscrapers in Futuristic Metropolis on page 100.

*Bonus Round*
Mini-fridge
Wastebasket
Athletic socks

# Luxe Helix

Like the twisted ladder of a DNA strand, this helix design is endlessly interesting. Its combination of straight lines and two interlocking curves provides both depth and motion to a simple stencil.

## BACKBONE TEE

Obsessed with the biology of the body, we were drawn to the idea of a helicoid shape as the matrix or fundamental backbone of our bodies. By repeating the pattern down the length of a T-shirt, it follows the central flow of life within the body.

**Segment 16,** *design collective*

The drier the paint, the more variations you will be able to achieve in line thicknesses on the fabric. It can become a nice design element.

A cotton canvas fabric makes a great choice for a sturdy bag and absorbs paint well. To avoid blotching, just be careful not to use too much paint on your brush.

**Ursula Gullow,** *designer*

With this surface, you won't have to worry about tape or adhesive sticking to the surface after you stencil. Just use thumbtacks or straight pins to secure the stencil to the cork. It's simple!

**Morris Shakespeare,** *designer*

# HELICORK

*Bonus Round*
Bench
CD holder
Shower door

# Paisley Pochoir

What exactly *is* paisley? Originally a Persian design, it's named after a textile mill town in Scotland. How about "pochoir"? That's a French word used to refer to stenciling as an artistic technique. Confused? Let's just skip the words and concentrate on these fabulous designs.

## MIX AND MATCH

It's a good idea to apply your main patterns—the paisley swirls—first and let them dry before stenciling on the small circles that complete the design. You can use the stencil or create your own "holey" stencil with contact paper and a hole punch.

**P.S.** The Colorful Palate Catering Company in Asheville, North Carolina, uses this pretty little mixer to make the best coconut butter cookies ever!

**Tyler Rogero,** *designer*

# GREEN DREAM

Adhere a large piece of craft paper to the back of the curtain using spray adhesive. You can move it to other positions on the curtain as you stencil.

Dab on the fabric paint with a makeup sponge. Once dry, heat set the fabric paint with an iron.

**Joan K. Morris,** *designer*

# DRESSED UP STEP UP

I love adding a bit of art to everyday objects. Don't you?

Changing the hue adds a touch of whimsy. Try matching or contrasting colors for a different look.

**Melissa Lichtenwald-Thomas,** *designer*

*Bonus Round*
Bathroom storage
Cabinets
Necktie

# Power Lines

In this post-modern urban landscape, all you see is what you usually ignore. Is it art? In the right hands, this deceptively stylish design can turn the commonplace into a conversation piece.

## CREATIVE ENERGY

Since I used a fabric mouse pad, I used fabric paint. I chose blue for the background to give the feeling of a sky.

I chose to duplicate the design, one on either side of the mouse pad, to create the feeling of an open road.

**Beth Harvey,** *designer*

# CURRENT CANDLESCAPE

The first time I attempted this project, I wrapped the lamp in contact paper, taped a paper template onto the lamp, and cut the stencil directly on the glass surface. Big mistake. When I lifted the parts out, they were hard to see. When I painted the stencil, the paint bled because of the frosted surface. All in all, it was a disaster.

Most sign shops sell small amounts of adhesive vinyl—it comes in a variety of colors, including metallics. Be sure to cut your stencil immediately after you apply it to the glass. The longer the vinyl is on the glass, the harder it is to remove.

**Terry Taylor,** *designer*

For this project, my goal was to make the design look worn, so that it appears as old as the suitcase itself.

I use the top case for paint supplies, so why not stencil it? I combined motifs and colors to complement the suitcase. Now I love taking it out!

You can match a paint color to the suitcase and use it to fill in the detail areas if the stencil smears.

**Ursula Gullow,** *designer*

*Bonus Round*

TV trays
Breaker box door
Kite

# Flash Dragon

Dragons inspire fantasy . . . and who doesn't want more fantasy in their lives? Place this fire-breathing design on just about anything and let it ignite your imagination.

I like the idea that these are flames that not even a downpour can douse.

The thicker the paint, the less it will bleed. Use an artist's brush for dynamic color blending.

**Ursula Gullow,** *designer*

FIRE & WATER

# DEEPEST DARKEST DIARY

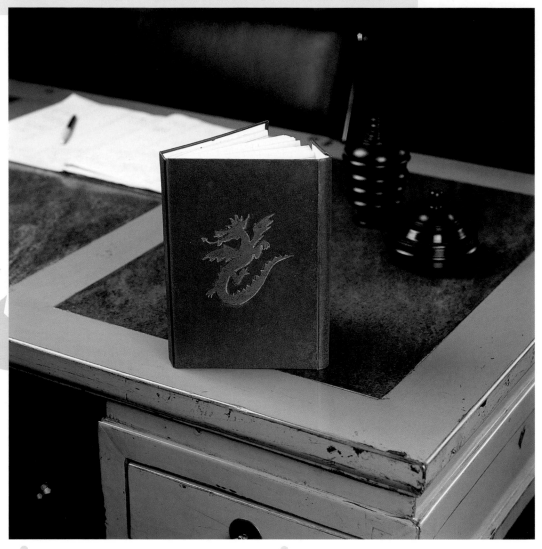

With all the fantasy books out there, I think it's very appropriate to have a dragon on a journal.

I used a flat plastic-covered sponge to lay on the dark brown glaze so that its wrinkles and lines emulated leather, and then I added a lighter second coat.

I imagined there was light raking across the dragon. With the glaze still wet, I used a lighter-colored pencil to outline the highlighted side and a darker pencil to outline the sides that fell into the shadows. Because the glaze is water-based, I sealed the journal after it was thoroughly dry.

**Beth Harvey,** *designer*

# SERPENT STONE

Find a light-colored river rock that's a good size for a doorstop. Wash it and let it dry overnight in a warm place.

A rock won't give you a perfectly flat surface to work with, so trace the design onto the front of some clear contact paper. Place the stencil on the rock, pressing down the edges. With outdoor paint and a makeup sponge, dab the paint on evenly. Carefully remove the stencil.

**Joan K. Morris,** *designer*

*Bonus Round*
Bandana
Karate uniform
Grill cover

# Poppies Aplenty

The poppy is a natural choice for stenciling because of its dramatic colors and voluptuous shape. Poppy flowers are usually portrayed as red but can also be white, pink, blue, orange, or yellow.

POPPYTALK

To apply a stencil on a rounded surface like the French press, you may need to paint the poppies one section at a time.

Enamel paints worked well on the glass.

**Tyler Rogero,** *designer*

To make sure my poppies lined up, I ran a piece of masking tape across the bottom of the chair back where I wanted the stems to end.

I used paints appropriate for metal and a very dry makeup sponge, removing most of the paint from the sponge before applying it to the stencil. For the flowers, I started with the yellow paint, and then dabbed on the red, black, and green.

Adding another stencil—in this case, the bee from page 61—rounded out my garden theme.

**Joan K. Morris,** *designer*

# SUMMER GARDEN CHAIR

# PANELS O' POPPIES

Enlarge your stencil five times or more for bold, extra-large poppies, and paint one per curtain panel.

These overgrown, exaggerated poppies made me think of a whimsical first apartment. With subtler colors, the curtains could suit any home. For a different look, try black and white paint on a bold background.

**Beth Harvey,** *designer*

Natural cotton dishtowels are often sold in sets. Stencil them all at once and tuck them away for last-minute hostess gifts … that is, if you can bear to part with them!

The linear quality of this stencil motif perfectly complements the printed pattern of the fabric.

**Tyler Rogero,** *designer*

# KITCHEN BLOOMS

*Bonus Round*
Hankies
Floor cushion
Lightswitch cover

# Grinning Skull

Punk, Goth, or just Halloween? This design can make people laugh out loud or shiver in fright, depending on how you use it. Don't wait–the clock is ticking!

## SILVER-PATED BROOCH

I made this silver brooch by sawing the shape of the skull and piercing the eyeholes. To make the teeth, I first cut straight across to get the general shape of the mouth, and then I sawed the individual spaces.

I created the final texture with a steel brush.

**Joanna Gollberg,** *designer*

# POOR YORICK BLAZER

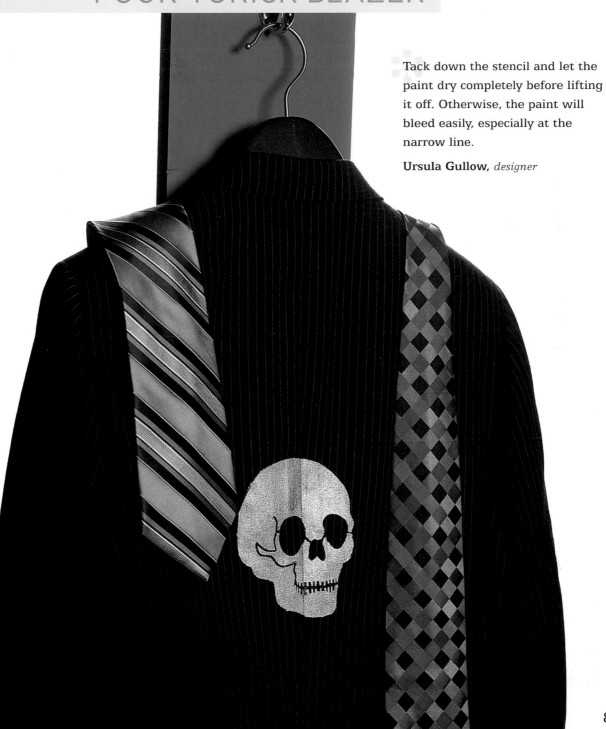

Tack down the stencil and let the paint dry completely before lifting it off. Otherwise, the paint will bleed easily, especially at the narrow line.

**Ursula Gullow,** *designer*

A project like this one is a great chance for experimenting with different paints: metallic, fluorescent … whatever you'd like.

**Melissa Lichtenwald-Thomas,** *designer*

The Remix
This skull also makes a spooky book cover decoration. See CosmiCovers on page 104.

*Bonus Round*
Tote for cleaning supplies
Welcome mat
Pumpkins

# Floating Jellyfish

Nature provides many stencil-able shapes, but who would have thought the foreboding jellyfish could be so beautiful? Yet its fluid form adds offbeat elegance to so many things.

## PINK STINGER

Using the dressmaking skills of Segment 16 member R. Brooke Priddy, we created this project as a natural flow of materials.

After enlarging the stencil, we painted directly on the outer layer of the dress. The tentacles are woven strips of synthetic fabrics dangling around the fringe.

**Segment 16,** *design collective*

# SAND AND SEA

You can stencil *anything*. How about taking a stencil down to the beach with you and stenciling the beach itself? Sift dry sand over a stencil on wet sand, or use your sand bucket to pour water over a stencil on dry sand. Maybe a crazy idea, but you won't know for sure until you try!

**Melissa Lichtenwald-Thomas,** *designer*

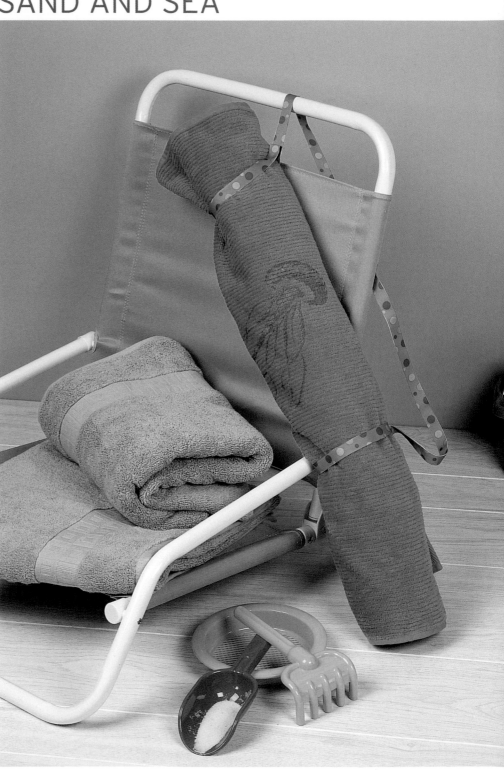

# TENTACLE TRAY

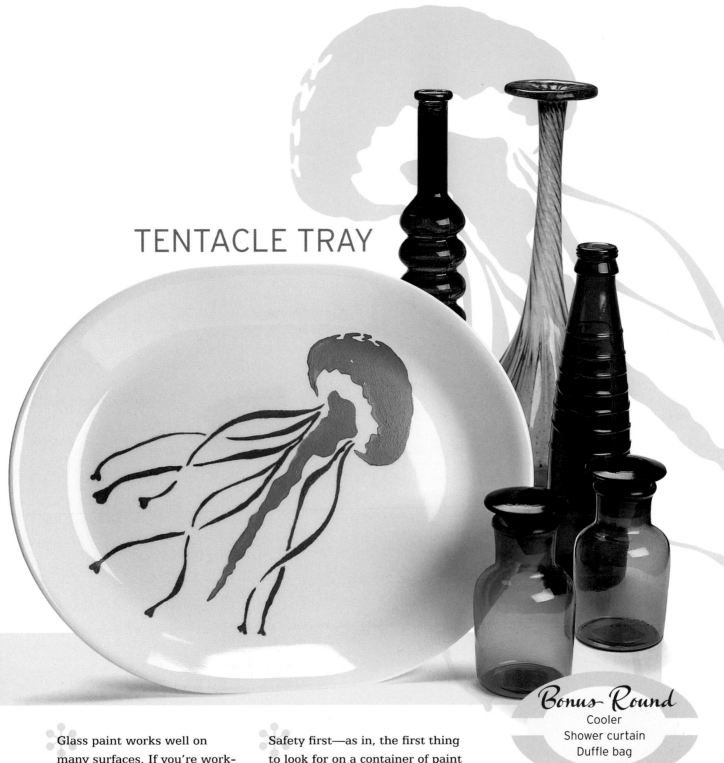

Glass paint works well on many surfaces. If you're working with a clear glass plate, consider a transparent glass paint that will let a little light shine through.

Safety first—as in, the first thing to look for on a container of paint for this project is whether or not it is dishwasher, microwave, and food safe.

**Tyler Rogero,** *designer*

**Bonus Round**
Cooler
Shower curtain
Duffle bag

# Jumping Jacks

Ah ... youth! Recess may no longer be part of your daily routine, but that's no reason to stop having fun. This design is a simple yet striking graphic icon that forever speaks of carefree days.

## JACKS FOR JILL CUFF

I fashioned this bracelet from a men's shirt cuff. I used the stencil to create a hand-stitched embroidered design.

The stitches to make this cuff are quite simple (just up and down) but each one requires attention. To make the jacks look realistic, straight lines are important, and it takes time to round the balls at the end.

**Morgan Purdy,** *designer*

92

# BOUNCING OFF THE WALLS

This theme will enliven the wall of any child's room. Painting the jacks in bold primary colors is another way you could go.

**Beth Harvey,** *designer*

The easiest way to stencil cupcakes is in reverse. Cut the design out of freezer paper and press it onto frosting that has not yet hardened. Roll the cupcake over a plate of sugar sprinkles and shake off the excess. Carefully remove the paper design with a toothpick or wooden skewer.

**Morris Shakespeare,** *designer*

# TOYSIES CHEST

It still may be a tough task to get kids to put their toys away, but I think this chest really does put the "fun" back in "functional."

**Tyler Rogero,** *designer*

**Bonus Round**
Sleeping bag
Sneakers
Sippy cup

# Red Coral

Are aquariums too much trouble to maintain? Why not paint your own underwater world? This design recalls deep dives and colorful coral. Use it as an accent or add simple fish to complete an aquatic ecosystem.

## SEA BATH

On ceramic pieces, it's best to use an oil paint, and then seal the paint with a ceramic sealer.

Here's how to give the coral some added texture: Lay on the base color and let it dry. Then using a natural sea sponge (very appropriate!) and a tint of the base color, dab on an accent color.

**Beth Harvey,** *designer*

I gave these stencils a drop shadow. After choosing your colors, start with the shadow color, painting it fully. Let the paint dry. Shift the stencil slightly over the first shape and apply the second color.

By changing fabric and switching the colors, I created matching placemats. That's the beauty and versatility of using drop shadows while stenciling.

**Beth Harvey,** *designer*

# Blast Off!

Space ... the final frontier. Let this design transport you to the outer galaxies of your imagination. A simple rocket ship can bring out the sense of wonder in all of us.

## POCKET ROCKET

Use glitter glue to make the dots and glitter spray to add sheen. You *want* people to notice your work!

You can use acrylic paint in lieu of fabric paint. Try both on a piece of scrap fabric and compare the results.

**Ursula Gullow,** *designer*

The Remix
Watch these rockets zoom above the skyline in Futuristic Metropolis on page 100.

# SPACE HOODIE

Be sure to wash the sweatshirt first. I stenciled the body of the rocket and the outline of the flame first, using black fabric paint and a makeup sponge. Just dab on the paint and carefully remove the stencil. Let it dry to the touch.

To make the flame, place the saved negative portion of the stencil over the painted tail. Use red fabric paint and a makeup sponge to paint the fire.

**Joan K. Morris,** *designer*

# MEDITATABLE

A well-chosen palette of neutral paints work together to create a very impressive, archaic feel.

Spend a little extra time wrapping the stencil around the table edge—precision pays off!

**Melissa Lichtenwald-Thomas,** *designer*

The technique used here produces a *pietre dure* effect. This art form, which means "hard stone" in Italian, uses tiny colored stones precisely cut and placed in a frame to create a mosaic. Artists began creating *pietre dure* pieces in Rome in the 1500s, but the technique became popular a century later in Florence. The designs ran the gamut from patterns (like this mandala) to complex portraits. The technique was also used in South Asia, where it was called *parchin kari*.

**Stephanie Brown,** *designer*

INTRICATE INLAY

*Bonus Round*
Wall clock
Headboard
Canisters

# PARTYING GIFT

A bottle of wine will taste better when presented in a custom felt gift bag.

A personalized hostess gift inspired this project. If you bring your friend a bottle of wine in this, your creativity will prove that it really is "the thought that counts." The best thing is: It's so easy!

I cut the stencil design out of the top layer of felt on this two-layer bag—sort of a reverse appliqué.

**Melissa Lichtenwald-Thomas,** *designer*

112

I enjoy breaking up patterns, which changes their overall look and feel. This design would make a great backsplash in a funky kitchen, but it could also hold its own as a hanging art piece.

After resizing the design, I inverted and flipped a few of the tiles. I also left some blank to make sure the composition wasn't too dizzying.

I used an oil paint so it won't peel, but you'll still have to be careful when handling the tiles. Use a ceramic sealer before grouting.

**Beth Harvey,** *designer*

CUBIST DREAM

*Bonus Round*
Pot rack
Sconce
Armoire

# INDEX